ISBN 978-1-332-93296-2
PIBN 10439512

1 MONTH OF
FREE
READING

at

www.ForgottenBooks.com

By purchasing this book you are eligible for one month membership to ForgottenBooks.com, giving you unlimited access to our entire collection of over 700,000 titles via our web site and mobile apps.

To claim your free month visit:

English
Français
Deutsche
Italiano
Español
Português

www.forgottenbooks.com

Mythology Photography **Fiction**
Fishing Christianity **Art** Cooking
Essays Buddhism Freemasonry
Medicine **Biology** Music **Ancient**
Egypt Evolution Carpentry Physics
Dance Geology **Mathematics** Fitness
Shakespeare **Folklore** Yoga Marketing
Confidence Immortality Biographies
Poetry **Psychology** Witchcraft
Electronics Chemistry History **Law**
Accounting **Philosophy** Anthropology
Alchemy Drama Quantum Mechanics
Atheism Sexual Health **Ancient History**
Entrepreneurship Languages Sport
Paleontology Needlework Islam
Metaphysics Investment Archaeology
Parenting Statistics Criminology
Motivational

MINUTES

OF THE

FORTY-FOURTH ANNUAL SESSION

OF THE

Shelby Baptist Association,

HELD WITH

Jemison Baptist Church, Chilton County, Alabama,

AUGUST 28th AND 29th, 1895.

———————— ✦ ————————

OFFICERS:

Rev. F. M. WOODS, Moderator................. ......Jemison, Ala.

Rev. C. W. O'HARA, Clerk and Treasurer....Columbiana, Ala.

———————— ✦ ————————

The next session of the Association will be held with Kingdom Church,
Shelby County, Alabama, four miles east of Columbiana,
commencing on Wednesday before the 1st
Sunday in September, 1896.

ORDER OF BUSINESS.

1. Devotional Exercises.
2. Introductory Sermon.
3. Read Letters from Churches.
4. Elect Moderator, Clerk and Treasurer.
5. Invite Visiting Ministers to Seats.
6. Invite Churches to join the Association.
7. Appoint Committees on Devotion, Finance and Nominations.
8. Fill Vacancies in Standing Committees.
9. Call for Correspondence.
10. Return Correspondence.
11. Miscellaneous Business.
12. Adjourn.

SECOND DAY.

13. Devotional Exercises.
14. Read the Minutes of the First Day and Call the Roll.
15. Report on Family Religion.
16. Report on Education.
17. Missions—State, Home and Foreign.
18. Missionary Sermon.
19. Report on Ministerial Education.
20. Report on Periodicals.
21. Report on Aged and Infirm Ministers.
22. Report on Bible and Colportage Work.
23. Report on Temperance.
24. Report on Sabbath Schools.
25. Report on Nominations.
26. Report on Finance.
27. Report of Treasurer.
28. Appoint Standing Committees to report at next session.
29. Order Clerk's Salary paid, and 500 Copies of Minutes printed.
30. Miscellaneous Business.
31. Adjourn.

MINUTES.

The Shelby Association met with Jemison Church, Aug. 28th, 1895.

Devotional exercises were conducted by J. E. Adams, who read the 23d Psalm, and prayers were offered by J. E. Adams, J. F. Averyt and H. C. Taul.

On motion, Rev. F. M. Woods was called to the chair, the former moderator, E. B. Teague, being absent.

Introductory sermon was preached by H. C. Taul, from Rom. 10th and 21st. At the suggestion of J. G. Harris, a song was sung, and the greeting hand was extended.

Adjourned until 2 p. m.

AFTERNOON SESSION.

The Association met pursuant to adjournment.

W. H. Connell read the 67th Psalm, and prayers were offered by N. T. Lucas and J. M. Crenshaw.

Letters from the churches were called for, received, read and the names of the messengers enrolled as follows :

FIRST DISTRICT.

Brierfield—L. P. Brock and P. A. Wood.
Bethlehem—Letter and Funds.
Cahaba Valley—T. M. Fancher, W. M. Kerbo and Curtis Crider.
Calera—Letter and Funds.
Dogwood Grove—W. S. Lovelady, W. Z. Lovelady, Derrick Lolly.
Enon—P. L. Lucas, N. T. Lucas, John Boyd.
Helena—J. D. Martin and T. L. Douglass.
Jemison—F. M. Woods, J. R. Hill and T. C. Fand.
Longview—Letter and Funds.

Montevallo—H. C. Reynolds and Wm. Lyman.
Mar's Hill—James Campbell and W. Poe.
Macedonia—Not Represented.
New Antioch—Not Repesented.
Six Mile—W. L. Tricks, Lawler Wells and F. H. Farington.

SECOND DISTRICT.

Bethesda—Letter and Funds.
Columbiana—C. W. O'Hara.
Center Hill—George W. Carter.
Florence—J. M. Crenshaw.
Kingdom—J. F. Hill and George Pitts.
Liberty—J. E. Adams, R. J. Ray.
Mt. Calvary—H. C. Tail and C. L. Mooney.
New Prospect—J. H. R. Carden and C. L. M. Fincher.
Rocky Ridge—John Atcherson and E. B. Davis.
Summer Hill—W. E. Price and W. D. Beardon.
Shelby—J. F. Averyt, M. F. Comer and W. A. Walker.

Proceeded to the election of moderator, clerk and treasurer by ballot, which resulted in the unanimous choice of F. M. Woods, Moderator ; and C. W. O'Hara, Clerk and Treasurer.

On motion, the order of business of the last session was adopted for the present.

Invited churches to join the Association. None.

Invited visiting brethren to seats.

Bro. J. G. Harris was received as representative of the Alabama Baptist.

Appointed committees :

On Devotional Exercises—Pastor and messengers of Jemison church.

On Finance—J. E. Adams, H. C. Reynolds and J. R. Fill.

On Nominations—T. M. Fancher, Wm. Lyman and J. F. Averyt.

Filled vacancies on standing committees :

On Periodicals—H. C. Reynolds, N. T. Lucas and R. J. Ray.

On Temperance—J. F. R. Carden, George W. Carter, M. F. Comer and J. M. Crenshaw.

Called for correspondence :

Rev. W. F. Connell and J. M. McCord were received from the

Birmingham Association: J. G. Farris from the Montgomery Association.

Returned Correspondence :

Cahaba Valley Association—J. H. R. Carden.
Unity Association—F. M. Woods and T. M. Fancher.
Weogufka Association—C. W. O'Hara and J. F. Averyt.
Coosa River Association—H. C. Taul and George W. Carter.
Birmingham Association—H. C. Taul.
Tuscaloosa Association—T. M. Fancher.

On motion the reports on State, Home and Foreign Missions, and on colportage work were made a special order for 10:30 a. m. Thursday, to be followed by a lecture on Missions, by J. G. Harris.

The report on Education was read and discussed by C. W. O'Hara, J. G. Harris, J. H. R. Carden, J. D. Martin and H. C. Reynolds. Report adopted.

REPORT ON EDUCATION.

To the Shelby Association : Your Committee on Education have not the necessary statistics at hand to make an intelligent report. From the best information we have there is lack of interest in the cause of education within our bounds. The attendance at Howard College is encouraging and the same is true of the Judson College, both of which we earnestly recommend to the prayerful consideration of the Baptists of the Shelby Association. We wish to emphasize the fact so often repeated to the Association,—that the demand for Christian men and women of strong minds and thorough cultivation is increasing, and that the cause of education, in our opinion, is not languishing, but increasing within our bounds, which is very gratifying considering the hard times. Respectfully submitted.

W. F. THOMPSON, } Committee.
R. H. PRATT.

Adjourned to 8:30 a. m. Thursday.

Preaching at night by J. H. R. Carden from Heb. 3d Chap. and part of 7th and 8th verses.

THURSDAY, Aug. 29, 1895.

Association met pursuant to adjournment.

Devotional exercises were conducted by T. M. Fancher.

Invited visiting brethren to seats. B. F. Giles, representing Howard College, and W. B. Crumpton representing S. B. of M. and the Judson Institute ; J. M. McCord, corresponding messenger from the Birmingham Association, and J. B. Kilpatrick, corresponding messenger from the Coosa River Association, were received.

Appointed a Memorial committee on the demise of Rev. J. W. Wood, viz : J. M. Crenshaw, H. C. Taul and T. M. Fincher.

The report on Family Religion was read and discussed by T. M. Fincher, J. H. R. Carden, J. B. Kilpatrick, W. B. Crumpton, J. M. McCord, F. H. Farrington, C. W. O'Hara and J. D. Martin. Report adopted.

REPORT ON FAMILY RELIGION.

Your Committee on Family Religion ask leave to report : We believe that according to the teachings of both the Old and New Testaments that the responsibility of instructing children in the ways of the Lord rests wholly upon parents. If this be true, how great, how solemn the responsibility. We do, therefore earnestly and prayerfully recommend to parents and heads of families the importance of teaching the Scriptures, and bring them up in the nurture and admonition of the Lord.   THOMAS M. FANCHER, Chairman.

The special order was taken up and the report on State Missions read. There being no report on Home Missions the clerk was authorized to insert Facts and Figures pertaining to Home Missions in the minutes.

The report on Foreign Missions was read.

The report on Colportage Work was read, and on motion for the adoption of these reports, the following discussions were had.

J. G. Harris delivered a lecture on the "Trials and Triumps of the Christian Religion."

Adjourned to 2 p. m.

AFTERNOON SESSION.

Association met. Devotional exercises were conducted by J. M. McCord.

On motion, the further consideration of State, Home and Foreign Missions reports were deferred and made a special order for the evening session.

The discussion of the report on Colportage Work was continued by H. C. Tiul, J. H. R. Carden, W. B. Crumpton and J. M. McCord. Report adopted.

REPORT ON BIBLE AND COLPORTAGE.

This work is to the minds of your committee one of the most important fostered by our denomination. Yet the most neglected. Important, 1st. Because of the need of the Bible and Baptist literature among our people.

2d. Through a colporteur we can supply this destitution.

3d. Through this channel of our work we reach the country, and do a missionary work that has been reached from no other source.

We have no colporteur in our Association, the result is many homes without Baptist books, and some cases without a good Bible and some none at all. About one year ago, Bro. Crumpton had printed in the Alabama Baptist the opinions of many of our leading pastors of the State on the work. They all felt and realized that a good result would follow the appointment of a good, active colporteur in each Association. Yet the minutes of the State convention for 1894 show that only nine out of the seventy-five (75) Associations in the State of Alabama have an active colporteur. Had we a good brother travelling in our midst, whose duties shall be to preach, sell books, and take collections for this department of our work, great good would result therefrom. With the right man in the field, our weak churches would be worked up, and the denomination would take on new life.   J. W. MITCHELL, Chairman.

The report on Ministerial Education was read and discussed by B. F. Giles.   The following pledges were made for Ministerial Education :

Bethlehem church	$ 3 00
Cahaba church	15 00
Cahaba Valley church	5 00
Columbiana church	10 00
Center Hill church............by G. W. Carter	50 pd
Dogwood Grove church	5 00
Helena church..............by J. D. Martin	50 pd
Mt. Calvary church	5 00
Six Mile church	5 00

Montevallo church.............................. .... 25 00
Liberty church................................... 10 00
Jemison church................................... 8 00 pd
J. A. Skaggs.................................... 3 00

Total...................... $119 00

J. B. Crumpton and J. G. Harris addressed the Association on the subject of Ministerial Education, Howard College and Judson Institute.   B. F. Giles represented the Howard.
Report on Ministerial Education adopted.

REPORT ON MINISTERIAL EDUCATION.

We deem it an altogether unnecessary task to undertake to instruct or advise this intelligent body of Christians (messengers and ministers from the churches of the Shelby Association) as to the pressing, yea, imperative demand, for an educated ministry. The evidence of this proposition is demonstrated by reference to the financial exhibit of the minutes of our last Association, which shows that more money was given for this cause than any other object fostered by the Association.

So it occurs to us that the main subjects of discussion should be first: "Who to Educate?" 2d. "The Ways and Means."

During the past year there were twenty-three young men in Howard College studying for the ministry. At the seminary seven from our State; six of the seven of these candidates for the seminary were graduates of Howard College, and its a gratifying fact that these six passed with credit every examination required by this grand school.

We would also express our pleasure at the good report we hear of our beneficiary Bro. J. W. O'Hara, who has been attending Howard College, and learn with joy of the good work he is doing, and commend him for it. In this connection we would call attention to the fact that it is almost universally the case, that these young men who are struggling to get an education so they may successfully devote their lives to the cause of Christ are generally those who owing to their adaptability and general character would be the most successful in the ordinary affairs of men, and we fear too often are forgotten by the brethren. We feel that the entire denomination is under deep and lasting obligations to the officers of our college for the sacrifices they are so continually making in aiding our young men who are studying for the ministry, and urge our brethren to give the college all possible support and encouragement.

Respectfully submitted.

H. C. REYNOLDS, Chairman.

On motion, the Moderator appointed a committee to examine Bro. F. H. Farrington, who has been recommended by Six Mile Church as a ministerial beneficiary, consisting of C. W. O'Hara, J. H. R. Carden, H. C. Taul and J. D. Martin.

The report on Periodicals was read and discussed by J. G. Harris, C. W. O'Hara, J. M. McCord, J. F. Averyt, J. H. R. Carden, H. C. Taul, T. M. Fincher, J. B. Kilpatrick, G. W. Carter, and J. M. Crenshaw. Report adopted.

Adjourned to 7:30.

EVENING SESSION.

Association met. The Moderator read the 2d Psalm, and prayer was offered by the Clerk.

Resumed the discussion of mission reports. Participated in by W. B. Crumpton, J. M. McCord, and C. W. O'Hara. Report on State Missions adopted.

REPORT ON STATE MISSIONS.

By a faithful working of State Missions a broad basis may be laid for Foreign Mission work, as many foreigners are flowing into our midst; especially in mining districts, and many of them return to their native country, or write and will necessarily report what is going on here; and, if we are doing a good work here it will be sure to establish the work of Foreign Missions there. From the best information we can obtain, the work of the State Board is very gratifying. In the first place, a great saving and convenience has been accomplished by the consolidation of the Board of Ministerial Education and colportage work, together with the State Mission work, known as the State Board of Missions, located at Montgomery in the same building with the Alabama Baptist. We have no report of State Mission work, later than the report of the short year (eight months) ending July 1894. By a careful review of the report we learn that the Board received for State Missions:

For State Missions.................. 4,736.62
Paid Missionaries............. ...... 3,102.04
On hand.... .... 106.53

Showing that the expenses of the Board was a little over fifteen hundred dollars, and that $846.50 of this expense was paid to the secretary of the State Board, who also works as missionary. We learn through the Alabama Baptist that Brethren A. E. Burns, A. J. Glenn, ind S. O. Y. Ray are doing good work as State Missionaries, also Bro. J. W. O'Hara is doing a good work, but not at the expense of the Board. And that Bro. W. B. Crumpton, our State secretary, is untiring in the work assigned him.

We would recommend that the Shelby Association heartily cooperate with the State Board of Missions. We learn from the corresponding secretary of the State Board that all is being done in the colporteur work that the stringency of the times will admit of. And that the State Board is helping the Home Board sustain a missionary among the colored people. Respectfully submitted,

J. D. MARTIN, Chairman.

Report on Home Missions, none.

FACTS AND FIGURES ON HOME MISSIONS.

The Home Board is striving to provide Gospel privileges for the vast number of foreigners coming into our Southland. This is a vast work. The United States census shows that in 1890 there were 9,121,867 who were born on foreign soil, 11,503,675 were born of foreign parentage. That means one out of every 6½ persons is a foreigner and that the influx is still increasing. God has brought the subjects of Foreign Missions to our doors. Shall we fail to give them the Gospel, as a means of their obtaining the bread of life? The demands upon us are the more pressing when we remember that foreigners bring with them anarchy, Romanism and want of morals. We must evangelize them, or they will overwhelm us.

The Indians need and demand our utmost diligence in giving them the Gospel. Much has been done for them, but much more remains to be done.

In Oklahoma and New Mexico, just now developing, the Board has a work of the utmost value and promise.

The native white population of the South in the mountain districts needs the Gospel. This the Board is endeavoring to supply.

The work in Cuba, which God has so wonderfully blessed, is now necessarily retarded by reason of war on the island.

The Negro—it is decided that the best thing to do for them is to teach and uplift their preachers. This is being attempted by institutes. The agreement of the joint committee composed of brethren South and North, at Fortress Monroe will bring the Colored Baptist Schools established by our Northern brethren nearer to the hearts of Southern Baptists, and it is to be hoped that much good will result therefrom.

It is gratifying to know of the improvement in the financial affairs of the Board. The report submitted to the S. B. C. one year ago showed an indebtedness of $6,500, and this year only $1,000. The perminent net assets of the Board have increased $5,500. The amount devoted to Church building was over $4,000. The number of the missionaries has been larger than any preceeding year, and the baptisms on the Mission Field have exceeded by over five hundred those of any other year in our history. These facts and figures should certainly stimulate us to greater activity and sacrifice for Home Missions.

Respectfully submitted,

C. W. O'HARA, Clerk.

Report on Foreign Missions adopted.

REPORT ON FOREIGN MISSIONS.

In our conception of Missionary enterprise as taught in the Word of God, it is a difficult matter to draw the line between Home and Foreign Missions. If there is taught in the Bible the duty to send the Gospel anywhere, there can no point be found at which it should stop. The whole world is the field, and we believe that the Baptist churches should send the Gospel to every part of this field, and think God that He thus allows us to labor for "Him that loved us." In order that we may have intelligent conception of the work of Foreign Missions we beg to append part of the report of the Committee on Foreign Missions at our last State Convention, as follows: .

"Our Papal Missions embrace Italy, Brazil, and Mexico. Bro. Taylor's latest report of the work in Italy indicates considerable progress in one or another direction. Number of baptisms, 38; members 372. While obsticles are great where Romanism has reigned for ages, and while our Missionaries have many seasons of grief they also have times of rejoicing. Wide seed-sowing is being done in Italy and the time of harvest will surely come. Bro. Eager says: 'In looking back over the year, we feel that we have reason to thank God and take courage.'

"In spite of the war in Brazil, which greatly disturbed the work there, we have much for which we can praise God. Baptisms, 159; members, 519.

"In Mexico, a comparatively large force of Missionaries under the direction of Bro. W. D. Powell, are earnestly at work. The year has been one of great blessing on this field. These statistics are full of interest and encouragement:

Number of	churches		37
"	"	out stations	14
"	"	baptisms	277
"	"	members	1,163
"	"	Sunday schools	23
"	"	scholars	375
Contributed to Foreign Missions			$ 311,75

"   to Home Missions............ 519 50
"   " other purposes....... .. . 1,737 27

"Our Pagan Missions are located in Japan, Africa and China.

"In Japan, Bro. McCollum (our McCollum), Mrs. McCollum and Bro. E. N. Walne and Mrs. Walne, with four native assistants, constitute our force in this great empire. The work was begun in 1889. One church and six stations." Baptisms, 9; members, 31. Bro. McCullum writes: 'The seeds sown have hardly had time to bear fruit, but there is much in the work to encourage us. I ask you to say to the brethren of the South that we do not plead for houses for ourselves, nor for school buildings, nor for church buildings; but we do plead for men—men to help us preach the gospel to nine million heathen at our doors.

"In Africa, we have 9 missionaries, 7 assistants, 5 churches, 166 members, 24 baptisms; contributions, $123.50. Bro. Newton says: 'The Lord is greatly blessing our work. To His name be all honor and praise. Pray for us that we may be full of the Spirit and power to succeed in saving souls.

"The China Missions are divided into three: Northern, Central and Southern. Bro. Pruitt of Northern China, says: 'God has blessed us, and we give thanks to his Holy Name.' One has said of Central China: 'We feel that God has not withheld His blessings from us.' Of Southern China it may truly be said: 'The Lord is with us—His cause is advancing." In the China Missions—churches, 13; baptisms, 222; membership, 1,066.

"Alumni Baptists contributed to Foreign Missions for the year ending April 30, 1894, $7,047.68—a fraction over seven cents per member. In addition to the above, is is pleasant to note that Women's Mission Societies contributed $1,170.00."

In this time of great depression, God is greatly blessing our work in all fields, with thankful hearts and usual hopes. Let us turn our faces to the future, lifting our eyes and hearts to God. Let us join our brethren hand in hand saying as we press forward, " Blessed be the Lord God, the God of Israel who only doeth wondrous things; and blessed be his glorious name forever, and let the whole earth be filled with His glory.   Respectfully submitted,

                              H. C. TAUL, Chairman.

The Report on Aged and Infirm Ministers was read and discussed by J. M. Crenshaw. A collection was taken. (See amount in report of Finance Committee.) Report adopted.

REPORT OF AGED AND INFIRM MINISTERS.

We, your committee on Aged and Infirm Ministers, ask leave to report the following: We find that there are only two beneficiaries of this Association—Brethren W. W. Armstrong and J. F. R. Carden. These brethren have labored and spent their lives in the bounds of this Association, in the Master's cause. We reccommend that a collection be taken for the benefit of these brethren before the close of this session of the Association.

R. A. WOOD, Chairman.

The following was adopted :

Inasmuch as by misunderstanding the Association has in hand $25.00 worth of property belonging to F. M. Woods, former Colporteur of the Association, viz: $9.55 in cash, which has been paid over to the Colporteur Board, and $14.45 in books, which is in the Treasurer's hands, therefore,

RESOLVED, That the Clerk be authorized to turn the books over to F. M. Woods and give him an order on the Colportage department for the $9.55.

The report on Temperance was read and discussed by W. B. Crumpton, J. M. Crenshaw, J. M. McCord, H. C. Taul, H. C. Reynolds, C. W. O'Hara, and Geo. W. Carter. Report adopted.

REPORT ON TEMPERANCE.

We, your committee beg leave to submit the following report: To say that Intemperance is the curse of the age, is putting it in its mildest form. Our law-makers of the State have done all they could to prevent the manufacture and sale of intoxicating drink, and still the diabolical trade goes on in the form of distilled liquors, fermented wines and different compounds called whiskies, and still the sale goes on in local option districts, and, still nearly all classes of our people are drinking it. The churches are confused by this demon and is losing its influence over the world on this account. It is high time that we should awake out of sleep and do something. We can not, neither need we attempt to control the "Blind Tiger," but let us control our members who patronize the "tiger." We, your committee suggest that this Association reccommend in strongest terms to the churches that they discipline their members promptly and in a Scriptural manner; who in any way, aid or abet this nefarious and sinful practice in opposition to the law of God, our country, or the morals of the youth. Respectfully submitted,

J. F. R. CARDEN, Chairman.

The report on Sunday Schools was discussed by J. F.

Averyt, J. H. R. Carden, T. M. Fincher and John Hill. Report adopted.

REPORT ON SUNDAY SCHOOLS.

To show how few members of the church who attend Sunday School in comparison to the number of communicants, we quote the following from the last Sunday School report to the State Convention: "There are about 109,000 communicants, 1,600 churches, 700 Sunday Schools with 30,000 scholars." These figures prove that there is not the interest shown in this important work that should be by the Baptists of Alabama. We recommend that this work be vigorously prosecuted by pastors, deacons, and laymen, till every church within our bounds shall have a live Sunday School, also that we use the literature published by the Sunday School Board at Nashville, Tenn., 1st. Because it is equal to any literature. 2d. Because there is a profit arising therefrom, which is appropriated to missions. The Sunday School Board has turned over to the Mission Board in the last year, about One Thousand Dollars. Thus we see how the Sunday school is helping to send the gospel to other nations. This work patiently and persistenly followed, will bring good results, and substitute love for hate and life for death.   Respectfully submitted,

J. F. AVERYT, Chairman.

The Committee appointed to examine F. H. Farrington, in reference to his call to the ministry, made the following report :

We, your Committee appointed to examine F. F. Farrington, pertaining to his call to the ministry report that we have carefully and thoroughly examined said Brother and are led to believe that he is called of God to preach the Gospel, and do hereby heartily reccommend him to the State Board of Missions as a proper subject to become a beneficiary of the Ministerial Fund of the denomination, as a student at Howard College.   C. W. O'HARA,

J. F. R. CARDEN,

J. D. MARTIN,

H. C. TAUL,

Committee.

Report adopted.

Report on Periodicals was read and discussed by J. G. Harris, W. B. Crumpton, C. W. O'Hara, J. M. McCord, Geo. W. Carter, and J. H. R. Carden. Report adopted.

13

REPORT ON PERIODICALS.

Your committee believes that the mass of our membership are in great need of that knowledge of the objects fostered by the Baptist, that can only be obtained by reading our denominational literature, and we are aware that our Baptist papers have but meager circulation in our bounds. Many churches are entirely without any religious paper. We would urge our brethren to take more interest in this direction, that we may thus have our sympathies roused for the objects for which our brethren are laboring so earnestly in all the world. We heartily recommend the Alabama Baptist to the confidence and support of our brethren, and for Sunday schools, Kind Words Lesson Series, at Nashville, Tenn. Our Mission Journal is worthy of support, giving much information on the subject of missions, that can not be obtained otherwise. Respectfully submitted,

H. C. TAUL, Chairman.

The Report on Nominations was read and discussed by J. R. Hill, T. M. Fincher, and C. W. O'Hara. Report adopted.

REPORT OF COMMITTEE ON NOMINATIONS.

For Executive Committee—Moderator and Clerk: J. F. Averyt, J. R. Hill, F. C. Reynolds, L. P. Arnold, and H. C. Taul.

To preach the Introductory Sermon—W. H. Connell, J. W. Mitchell, alternate.

To preach the Missionary Sermon—E. B. Teague, C. W. O'Hara, alternate.

Delegates to the S. B. Convention—F. M. Woods, C. W. O'Hara, alternate.

Delegates to the State Convention—J. F. Averyt, W. H. Connell, C. W. O'Hara, T. M. Fincher, F. C. Reynolds, J. D. Martin, J. M. Crenshaw, William Lyman, J. E. Adams, George Stone, F. C. Taul, I. N. Langston, and F. M. Woods.

That the next session of the Association be held with Kingdom Church, commencing on Wednesday before the first Sunday in September, 1896. Respectfully submitted,

THOMAS M. FANCHER, Chairman.

REPORT ON FINANCE.

We, your committee on Finance submit the following report:

To amount received for minutes....................................$31 10
"   "   "   " Association purposes.................. 12 10
"   "   "   " State missions........................ 1 85
"   "   "   " Home   " 9 89

			"	Foreign "	....	2 54
			"	Ministerial education	....	10 75
			"	Indigent Ministers....	....	1 30
				collection for indigent ministers	....	9 62

Total.................................. ...$79 15

To amount paid over to treasurer......... ....$79 15

Respectfully submitted,
JAMES E. ADAMS, Chairman.

Report adopted.

REPORT OF TREASURER.

C. W. O'Hara in account with Shelby Association for the year 1894–95 :

DR.

Aug. 30, 1894. To balance last report......................... $57 50

Sept. 10, " " amt. recd. from Calera church for minutes..... 1 50

" 3, " " " " " Shelby ch for indigent min.... 2 55

Total..................................... ...$61 55

CR.

Sept. 3, 1894. By amt. pd. W. B. Crumpton S. missions.....$ 4 60

" " " " " " " " " Home missions..... 2 40

" " " " " " " " " Foreign " 4 00

" " " " " " " " " Min. education..... 5 50

Oct. 9, " " " " J. W. Wood, indigent min. ... 2 15

" " " " " " W. W. Armstrong, Indg't min.. 2 15

" " " " " " J. F. R. Carden, " " ... 2 15

Nov. 19, " " " " J. W. Wood, " " . 85

" " " " " " W. W. Armstrong, " " ... 85

" " " " " " J. F. R. Carden, " " ... 85

By amt. for postage during the year......... 1 20

" " " printing minutes.............. .. 20 00

" " " blank association letters........ 50

" " " clerk's salary.................... 14 35

$61 55

FOR THE YEAR 1895-96.

Aug. 30, 1895. To amt. received from finance committee.......$79 15

Respectfully submitted,
C. W. O'HARA, Treasurer.

Report adopted.

Appointed Standing Committees to report at the next session :

On Family Religion—J. E. Adams, A. F., Carden, and W. A. Jackson.

On Education—J. L. Peters, W. T. O'Hara, and E. C. Parker.

On Ministerial Education—J. F. Averyt, W. R. Craig, and S. J. May.

On Periodicals—J. R. Fill, T. C. Fand, and E. G. Givhan.

On Aged and Infirmed Ministers—J. M. Crenshaw, Geo. W. Carter, and J. R. Davis.

On State Missions—J. W. Mitchell, F. F. Farrington, and W. L. Trucks.

On Home Missions—H. C. Taul, N. Thomas, and A. J. Shaw.

On Foreign Missions—R. H. Pratt, Lawler Wells, and H. C. Owens.

On Temperance—H. C. Reynolds, William Lyman, and John McDonough.

On Sabbath Schools—T. M. Fincher, Geo. F. Farper, and Errick McGuire.

On Bible and Colportage Work—J. D. Martin, W. C. Denson, and T. L. Douglass.

RESOLVED, That the Clerk superintend the printing of 500 copies of minutes of this Association, and receive for his services as Clerk and Treasurer, the sum of $20.00.

RESOLVED, That this Association return its thanks to the people of this community for their hospitality, and pray God's blessings on them.

Adjourned.

F. M. WOODS, Moderator.

C. W. O'HARA, Clerk.

NOTICE.

We earnestly and respectfully request that the Messengers to the next session will come to stay until the close. We need three days.

F. M. WOODS, Moderator.

C. W. O'HARA, Clerk.

MINISTERS ORDAINED.

N. T. Lucas.................................. Montevallo, Alabama.
N. J. Jarvis............................ ....Dogwood, "
Charles Johnson............................Montevallo, "
J. W. Whitfield............................Columbiana, "
I. N. Walker..... ....Montevallo, "
F. C. Tull.......................................Pelham, "
J. D. Martin.....................................Pelham, "
W.W. Armstrong..............................Wilsonville, "
J. C. Lyon.................................... "
E. B. Teague........................... ......Columbiana, "
C. W. O'Hara................................ "
W. W. Kirkland.....................................Cresswell, "
J. D. Mills.......................................Gurnee, "
J. H. R. Carden.................................Weldon, "
B. C. Hughes.......................... "
J. W. Mitchell.................................Six Mile, "
W. H. Connell .... "
F. M. Woods.....................................Jemison, "
T. J. Parker..................................Columbiana, "
G.W. Crumpton.............................. "

LICENTIATES.

W. M. Kerbo...................... ...:..........Furnace, Alabama.
James Davis.....................................Columbiana, "
Thomas Davis................................. " "
I. J. Davis..................................... "
G. W. Moore......... .... "
J. F. Smith................................. ....Lewis. "
T. J. Cabaniss.......................................Lewis, "
F. F. Farrington.................................Six Mile. "

IN MEMORIAM.

Elder James Washington Wood was born March 2, 1822; died December 14, 1894, aged 72 years, 9 months and 12 days. He professed faith in Christ and was baptized into the fellowship of Mt. Hope church, Merriweather county, Georgia, at the age of 16, and was licensed by said church to preach the Gospel November 30, 1850. He moved to Tallapoosa county, Alabama, and was married to Mary Frances Murphy on the 30th of October, 1851. He was ordained to the full work of the ministry by Dry's Gap church, Bibb county, Alabama, on April 11, 1875. He was a faithful and devoted servant of the Master. He was the pastor of Rocky Ridge church for a number of years. A valiant soldier of the cross and delighted to sing that grand old Gospel hymn, "Am I a Soldier of the Cross, etc."

J. M. CRENSHAW.

STATISTICS OF SHELBY ASSOCIATION, 1895.

CHURCH.	COUNTY.	PASTOR.	CLERK.	CLERKS' P. O.	Membership last reported.	INCREASE BY				DECREASE BY				Pres. Membership	SUNDAY SCHOOL.		SUPERINTENDENT'S NAME AND POST OFFICE ADDRESS	Preaching Sabbaths.	Reports of Prayer-Meeting.	Reports Revival.
						Baptism.	Letter.	Voucher or Statement.	Restoration	Letter.	Exclusion.	Erasure.	Death.		Officers and Teachers.	Pupils.				
FIRST DISTRICT.																				
Brierfield.	Bibb.	J. W. Mitchell.	L. P. Brock.	Ashby.	39	2	3			15				31	2	25	John McDonough, Bismark	2		
Bethlehem.	Shelby.	W. H. Connell.	J. W. Arnold.	Bismark.	26	2	7				5	8		16	4	25	B. R. Owens, Six Mile.	2		1
Cahaba Valley.	Bibb.	"	E. R. McGuire.	Six Mile.	19	22	11							14½	6	40	D. W. Boyd, Calera.	4		1
Calera.	Shelby.		A. R. Scott.	Calera.	19		6							38	6	40				
Dogwood Grove.	Bibb.	R. E. Giles.	R. E. Wooley.	Dogwood.	118	19	12		1	1				131	7	53	P. L. Lucas, Montevallo.	2		1
Ebon.		J. W. Mitchell.	E. Daniel.	West Calera.	45	6	2							55						
Helena.		J. D. Martin.	H. W. Bowers.	Helena.	67	13	6		3	5	4		1	47	7	51		1		1
Jemison.	Chilton.	H. W. Woods.	T. C. Hand.	Jemison.	81	13	13			2	2			127	8	65	T. C. Hand, Jemison.			
Longview.	Shelby.	F. M. Woods.	C. E. Hale.	Longview.	49		4		1	1				53	10	65	William Lyman, Montevallo.	2		1
Montevallo.		A. W. McGaha.	C. E. Meroney.	Montevallo.	100	4	3							100				4		
Macedonia.			C. L. Walker.		42									42						
New Antioch.		Not represented	W. T. Walker.		125	1	6			9	4			112	7	25	L. M. Wells, Six Mile.	1	Weekly	1
Six Mile.		W. H. Connell.	Shelby Booth.	Gurnee.																
	Bibb.		L. M. Wells.	Six Mile.																
SECOND DIST'T.																				
Bethesda.	Shelby.	H. C. Taul.	R. A. O'Hara.	Wilsonville	104	5				10				97	8	51	J. C. Lyon, Wilsonville	1	Weekly	1
Columbiana.		E. B. Teague.	J. L. Peters.	Columbiana	62	2		1		6	2			57			W. L. Davis, Columbiana.	2	"	1
Center Hill.		C. B. Hughes.	W. G. Hardy.	Wilsonville.	46	3				5	2			44				4	"	
Florence.		Geo. Crampton.	J. M. Crenshaw	Lewis.	44	1	2			4				60				3	Irregular	1
Kingdom.		G. M. Lowrey.	A. F. Templin.	Columbiana	23	13								56			J. F. Crane, Weldon.	2	Monthly.	
Liberty.		C. W. O'Hara.	A. F. Carden.	Weldon	120									134	6	50	J. F. Crane, Weldon.	2	Irregular	1
Mars' Hill.	Jefferson.	A. F. O'Hara.	W. J. Nunally.	Helena.	57	1		1		5	2			51	3	25	W. J. Nunally, Helena.			
Mt. Calvary.	Shelby.	H. C. Taul.	W. L. Mooney.	Lynch.	54	2				2				58				2		
New Prospect			W. C. Carden.	Weldon	39	1				1	2			27				4	Weekly	1
Rocky Ridge.		Geo. Crampton	W. M. Davis.	Columbiana	55	13	3			2				77				2	Weekly.	1
Sumner Hill.			L. Q. Gould.	Columbiana	55	3	4			1				52				4	Weekly	1
Shelby.		C. W. O'Hara.	G. H. Averyt.	Shelby	65									55	8	50	J. F. Averyt, Shelby.	1	Weekly.	
Totals.					1478	134	95	10	12	103	90	15	16	1518	72	533				

† Churches not represented; former clerk and membership given.

FINANCIAL EXHIBIT OF SHELBY ASSOCIATION, 1895.

CHURCHES.	State Missions. (Voucher)	Home Missions. (Voucher)	Foreign Missions. (Voucher)	Baptist Orphanage. (Voucher)	Indigent Ministers. (Cash)	Indigent Ministers. (Voucher)	Ministerial. (Cash)	Ministerial. (Voucher)	Howard College Buildings. (Voucher)	Theological Seminary. (Voucher)	Judson Institute. (Voucher)	Incidental. (Voucher)	Minutes.	Associational Purposes.	School Expenses.	Total.	Pastor's Salary.	Repairs, Fuel, Poor, Etc.	Value of Buildings and Furniture.
	$6 50	$4 25	$3 20	2 13									$ 50	$1 00		$ 13 33	$ 69 00		$1011 00
			1 00										70			1 70			400 00
illey.	6 75	4 75		14 45								$ 6 50	3 00		$ 6 30	10 78	28 50	$ 21 00	1500 00
a,	10 00	6 75	5 00					†16 80	$ 5 00				1 75	60	10 00	45 45	150 00		400 00
ll,	1 50	2 00	†24 55	1 12									2 65	50	7 80	20 55	70 00	215 00	1200 00
rove.										$30 00		1 10	1 00			46 71	130 00		75 00
			1 90										1 00			4 10			400 00
		1 00											75	50	3 50	1 50			150 00
	1 00			2 05			$ 8 00	8 00				34 25	1 50	1 00		7 59	50 00	9 00	1000 00
													1 50			1 00			300 00
	12 50		5 00									47 00	50	1 00	12 00	4 00			700 00
											$25 00	7 00	3 00	50		91 30	50 00		300 00
																1 50			3200 00
		23 00	24 00	33 00				25 00				85 45	1 00	3 00	6 48	¶238 45	152 00	31 50	200 00
y.	20 00	1 70	50										2 00			15 33			200 00
ert.	5 15	2 36														4 36			300 00
ch.		50											50			1 00			200 00
ge.					9 62	$ 95		1 75				7 00	1 75	1 25	6 00	3 95	15 00	16 00	1000 00
lill	3 00	2 90	4 90										1 00	1 00		27 55			200 00
	16 55	6 50	7 00	1 00		2 57		10 00				8 00	1 75	50	22 32	76 47	85 00	10 00	1500 00
at Association.													2 50			9 62			
Totals.	82 95	48 19	77 14	53 75	9 62	3 42	8 00	61 64	5 00	20 00	25 00	196 30	31 85	11 60	74 40	698 99	810 50	302 50	15835 00

† $6.58 paid by Sunday School.   ‡ $2.36 paid by Sunday School.   ¶ Of this amount the Ladies' Aid Society paid $13.80, Sunbeams $30.00, Sunday

2.50.   § $30.00 of this amount was paid by the Sunday School.